11/06

STARS in the SPOTLIGHT

Kelly Clarkson

Colleen Adams

New York

Published in 2007 by The Rosen Publishing Group, Inc.
29 East 21st Street, New York, NY 10010

Book Design: Haley Wilson

Photo Credits: Cover © Dave Hogan/Getty Images; pp. 4, 18, 26 © Kevin Winter/Getty Images; p. 6 © Vince Bucci/Getty Images; p. 8 © Mark Mainz/Getty Images; p. 10 © Robert Mora/Getty Images; p. 12 © Kevin Winter/ImageDirect/FOX; p. 14 © Kevin Winter/ImageDirect; p. 16 © Scott Gries/ImageDirect; p. 20 © Scott Gries/Getty Images; p. 22 © STR/AFP/Getty Images; p. 24 © Frazer Harrison/Getty Images; p. 28 © Amanda Edwards/Getty Images.

Library of Congress Cataloging-in-Publication Data

Adams, Colleen.
  Kelly Clarkson / Colleen Adams.
      p. cm.
  Includes index.
  ISBN-13: 978-1-4042-3515-9
  ISBN-10: 1-4042-3515-9
  1. Clarkson, Kelly, 1982-—Juvenile literature. 2. Singers—United States—Biography—Juvenile literature. I. Title.
  ML3930.C523A65 2007
  782.42164092—dc22
  [B]
                                    2006015702

Manufactured in the United States of America

Contents

4

Kelly's Gift

Kelly Clarkson is best known as the winner of the first *American Idol: Search for a Superstar* in 2002. It is a national singing **competition** shown on the FOX television network. Kelly gained popularity after her win and had many opportunities to perform in front of large **audiences**. She won a million-dollar recording contract with RCA Records. Since then, she has successfully written and cowritten songs on two albums and is working on a third one. She won two Grammy Awards in 2006. Kelly has shown she has the talent and drive to make it big in the music business.

Kelly has a gift for songwriting and singing. She is shown here holding the two Grammy Awards she won in 2006.

Family Life

Kelly Brianne Clarkson was born in Fort Worth, Texas, on April 24, 1982. She was the third and youngest child in her family. Kelly's mom and dad separated when she was 6 and later got divorced. Her brother and sister went to live with other family members. Kelly stayed with her mom. They moved around to different places in Texas. Kelly's mom met and married Jimmy Taylor. The three settled in Burleson, Texas. Kelly said that her hit song "Because of You" is about dealing with her parents' divorce.

Kelly is shown here with her mom at a party after the 2004 Grammy Awards in Hollywood, California.

8

The School Choir

When she was young, Kelly wanted to be a **marine biologist**. After she saw a scary movie about sharks, she changed her mind. Kelly was asked to join the school **choir** in seventh grade when a teacher overheard her singing in the hall. She continued singing and performing in musicals throughout high school. As a member of the Texas All-State Choir, she received top honors for her singing ability. Kelly graduated from Burleson High School in 2000 and decided to **pursue** a career in music. She worked many different jobs to earn enough money to make a **demo** CD of her songs.

Kelly's hard work and faith in her talent would finally lead her to a career in music.

9

Chasing a Dream

Kelly had no luck selling her CD to record companies. She decided to move to Hollywood, California, with a friend. She hoped to find a record company that liked her music. When she didn't hear from any of the record companies, she looked for other jobs to earn money. Kelly appeared as an **extra** on the television show *Sabrina the Teenage Witch*. When she met famous songwriter Gerry Goffin, Kelly hoped he could help her get a recording contract. But then, many things went wrong. Goffin became ill. Kelly's roommate moved away, and their apartment burned down. After 4 months in Hollywood, Kelly moved back home to Texas.

Kelly thought she would have to give up her dream of becoming a recording artist when she left California.

Back Home

Kelly was disappointed that her dreams didn't come true in Hollywood. She decided to stay in Burleson and work as a waitress. One of Kelly's friends encouraged her to **audition** as a **contestant** for *American Idol: The Search for a Superstar*. The winner would receive a million-dollar recording contract with RCA Records. Kelly entered the contest for fun. After many auditions, she was selected by the show's three judges as one of the top thirty contestants. Every week, each contestant performed a new song for a national television audience. At the end of every show, viewers called in and voted for the person they thought gave the best performance.

It is estimated that more than 25 million viewers watched Kelly and other contestants on *American Idol* each week in 2002.

13

A Winner

Each week contestants were dropped from the *American Idol* contest. Kelly's warm personality and easygoing manner made her popular with viewers. She continued to receive votes for her singing performances and stayed in the contest. Finally, she made it to the top ten finalists. At the end of the competition, there were just two finalists left—Kelly and Justin Guarini. On September 4, 2002, Kelly won the contest with 58 percent of the audience votes. She sang a special song called "A Moment Like This," which was written especially for the *American Idol* winner.

Kelly and Justin Guarini are shown here at the *American Idol* finals in Los Angeles, California.

A Career in Music

When Kelly won the *American Idol* contest, it changed her life. RCA released Kelly's first single, "A Moment Like This," shortly after the contest ended. This song set a record when it climbed from number 52 to number 1 on the radio charts within a week. As a result of her popularity, Kelly received offers to do live performances and national tours. Kelly, Justin Guarini, and other *American Idol* finalists traveled throughout the United States on a sold-out tour. With a new recording contract, Kelly was also busy working on songs for her first album.

Kelly and Justin are shown here at the 2002 MTV Video Music Awards with *American Idol* judges Simon Cowell (far left), Paula Abdul (middle), and Randy Jackson (far right).

Thankful

Kelly's first album, *Thankful,* was released in April 2003. It sold more than 2 million copies in the United States. A song called "Miss Independent," written by Kelly and singer Christina Aguilera, became a big hit. This song showed Kelly's talent as a singer, songwriter, and recording artist. "Miss Independent" reached the top 10 on the charts. Clarkson was **nominated** in 2004 for a Grammy for the Best Female Pop Vocal for this song. Another song from *Thankful* was "The Trouble with Love Is." This song was featured in a movie called *Love Actually* in 2003.

Kelly is shown here singing to the audience after she won the *American Idol* contest in 2002. Shortly after winning, she recorded songs for her first album, *Thankful.*

From Justin to Kelly

After the success of the first season of *American Idol*, Kelly and Justin Guarini were chosen to star in a movie. *From Justin to Kelly* is a **comedy** about a group of college kids who meet in Florida during spring break. Kelly plays the role of Kelly Taylor, a singing waitress. Justin Guarini plays the role of Justin Bell, a college student from Pennsylvania. Kelly and Justin meet and like each other but unusual events keep them apart. Kelly, Justin, and their friends have fun singing and dancing on the beach.

From Justin to Kelly was filmed in Miami Beach, Florida, in 6 weeks. It came out in theaters in 2003.

Kelly in the Spotlight

Kelly's win as the first *American Idol* also led to many other performing opportunities. In December 2003, Kelly took part in a singing competition in London, England, called *World Idol*. She competed against winners from other national *Idol* shows from around the world. There were eleven judges, one from each country represented. Viewers in each of the countries called in and voted for their favorite singer. Kurt Nilsen from Norway won the competition with 106 points. Kelly took second place with 97 points. Kelly became known worldwide for her powerful voice.

Kelly Clarkson (back row–4th from the left) and Kurt Nilsen (back row–5th from the left) are shown here with the other *World Idol* contestants.

23

Breakaway

Kelly's second album, *Breakaway*, was released in November 2004. The songs on *Breakaway* were a change from pop music to rock music. Kelly cowrote six of the twelve songs on the album. One of these was the title song—"Breakaway"—which Kelly wrote with singer-songwriter Avril Lavigne. This song was a number-1 hit on the charts. It became even more popular when it was used in the **sound track** for the movie *The Princess Diaries 2: Royal Engagement*. Four of the songs from *Breakaway* were top 10 singles in the United States. This album sold more than 5 million copies in the United States.

Kelly is shown arriving at *The Princess Diaries 2: Royal Engagement* opening held at Downtown Disneyland in Anaheim, California.

Hit Songs

It is unusual for five songs on a single album to become hit songs. Kelly is the first recording artist to have two songs in the top 3 of the radio charts at the same time. These songs are "Since U Been Gone" and "Behind These Hazel Eyes." "Since U Been Gone" was the most successful single on the album. It reached number 2 on the radio pop charts in the United States and number 5 in the world. Other singles from *Breakaway*— "Behind These Hazel Eyes" and "Because of You"—were also on the top-10 charts. A fifth single from *Breakaway*, called "Walk Away," made it to the top 20 on the charts.

Kelly is shown here holding the People's Choice Award for Top Female Performer, which she won in 2006. Kelly has also won two American Music Awards and two MTV Awards for her music.

On the Road

Kelly and another *American Idol* favorite, Clay Aiken, toured the United States. This was Kelly's first major tour as a **solo** artist. Since then, Kelly has been on several tours in the United States and other countries. She said that being on the road often inspires her to write new songs. Kelly's concert tour to twenty-four cities in the summer of 2006 was called the "Addicted Tour." She likes traveling to different places so that fans can enjoy their old favorites and hear her new songs.

The "Addicted Tour" was Kelly's ninth tour in 2 years. She said that she loves touring because she loves her fans.

Much More to Come

In just a few years, Kelly has established a successful singing career. She said she was honored when asked to perform at the Grammy Awards in 2006. She never dreamed that she would receive two Grammy Awards that night. The first was for the Best Female Vocal Performance for the song "Since U Been Gone." The second was for Best Pop Vocal Album for *Breakaway*. Kelly said that winning was an unbelievable experience. But this is just the beginning of a long, successful music career for Kelly. Her friends and fans can't wait to see what she will do next.

Glossary

audience (AW-dee-uhns) A group of people gathered to see or hear something.

audition (aw-DIH-shun) A performance that tests the ability of an actor, singer, musician, or dancer.

choir (KWYR) A group of people who sing together.

comedy (KAH-muh-dee) A funny story that has a happy ending.

competition (kahm-puh-TIH-shun) A contest in which all who take part compete for the same thing.

contestant (kuhn-TEHS-tuhnt) Someone who takes part in a contest and competes against others.

demo (DEH-moh) A recording made to show off a song or performer to a record company.

extra (EHK-struh) A person hired to act in a group scene in a movie or television show.

marine biologist (muh-REEN by-AH-luh-jist) A scientist who studies animals and plants that live in the sea.

nominate (NAH-muh-nayt) To choose a candidate for election, appointment, or honor.

pursue (puhr-SOO) To find a way to accomplish.

solo (SOH-loh) Relating to something featuring or done by one person.

sound track (SOWND TRAK) The music for a movie or television show.

Index

A
"Addicted Tour," 29
Aguilera, Christina, 19
Aiken, Clay, 29
album(s), 5, 17, 19, 25
American Idol, 5, 13, 15, 17, 21, 23, 29

B
"Because of You," 7, 27
"Behind These Hazel Eyes," 27
Breakaway, 25, 27, 30

F
Fort Worth, Texas, 7
FOX television network, 5
From Justin to Kelly, 21

G
Goffin, Gerry, 11
Grammy Awards, 5, 19, 30
Guarini, Justin, 15, 17, 21

H
Hollywood, California, 11, 13

L
Lavigne, Avril, 25
Love Actually, 19

M
"Miss Independent," 19
"Moment Like This, A," 15, 17

P
Princess Diaries 2, The: Royal Engagement, 25

R
RCA Records, 5, 13, 17
recording contract, 5, 11, 13, 17

S
Sabrina the Teenage Witch, 11
"Since U Been Gone," 27, 30

T
Texas All-State Choir, 9
Thankful, 19
tour(s), 17, 29
"Trouble with Love Is, The," 19

W
"Walk Away," 27
World Idol, 23

Web Sites

Due to the changing nature of Internet links, PowerKids Press has developed an online list of Web sites related to the subject of this book. This site is updated regularly. Please use this link to access the list:
http://www.powerkidslinks.com/stars/clarkson/